ANIMAL FORMS

Collected and arranged by

NIGEL BILLINGTON AND JOHN JEFFERY

Design Centre, Pocklington School, York

Longman
London and New York

How to use the resource material

All the illustrations in this book are from nineteenth century
steel engravings.

Examples of interpretation and stylisation

The following sequences are examples of the way these illustrations can
be used to develop a design.

1

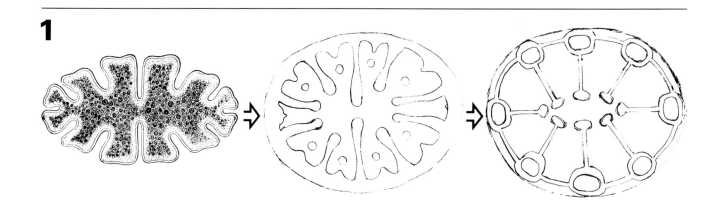

Starting with the image on page
59 of *Plant Forms* (the
companion volume).
The following three sketches were
made, in the order shown, during
the development of the etched
copper bowl design.

First sketch
The first sketch from the
engraving develops the outline
shape, emphasising the
indentations. The single circle in
each arm is suggested by the
apparently globular texture of the
engraving.

Second sketch
The circles have been moved into
the gaps and developed into a
decorative perimeter, suggesting
mounted gemstones, cloisonné
enamel or relief clay work in a
ceramic dish.

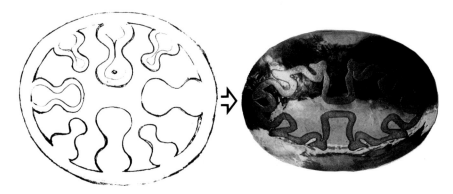

Third sketch
The circles and gaps have fused
into an hour-glass shape. In the
top part of the sketch an inner
pattern has been developed.

Etched copper bowl
Although the etched design is
very similar to the third sketch,
note that this final interpretation
is more 'flowing' and 'leafy'.

2

Using the fish image on page 25.

First sketch
The first sketch is similar to the original illustration but breaks up the picture into clearly defined black and white areas.

Second sketch
The fins have been stylised and the lines and circles representing them are repeated on the body of the fish.

Cold cast resin table top
The second sketch has been simplified to form the final design.

3 Using other images from the Design Resources:

Pelor filamentosum, page 24

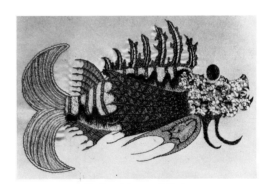

Embroidery of fish

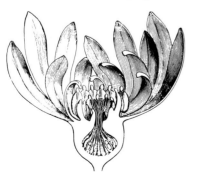

Calycanthus cut longitudinally, page 42 of *Plant Forms*

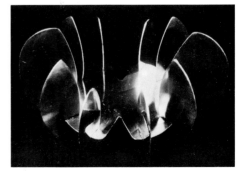

Nickel–silver centrepiece

The hoopoe, page 29

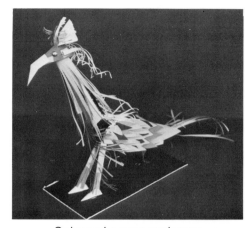

Coloured paper sculpture

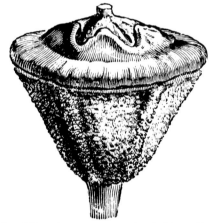

Stag beetle, page 41

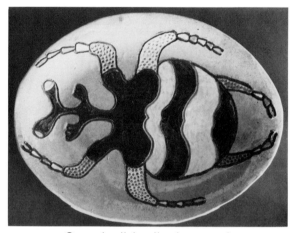

Ceramic dish, slip decorated

Fruit of Eucalyptus, page 1 of *Plant Forms*

Experimental card mock-up

Flower of broad-leaved Helleborine, page 53
of *Plant Forms*

Resin mat design

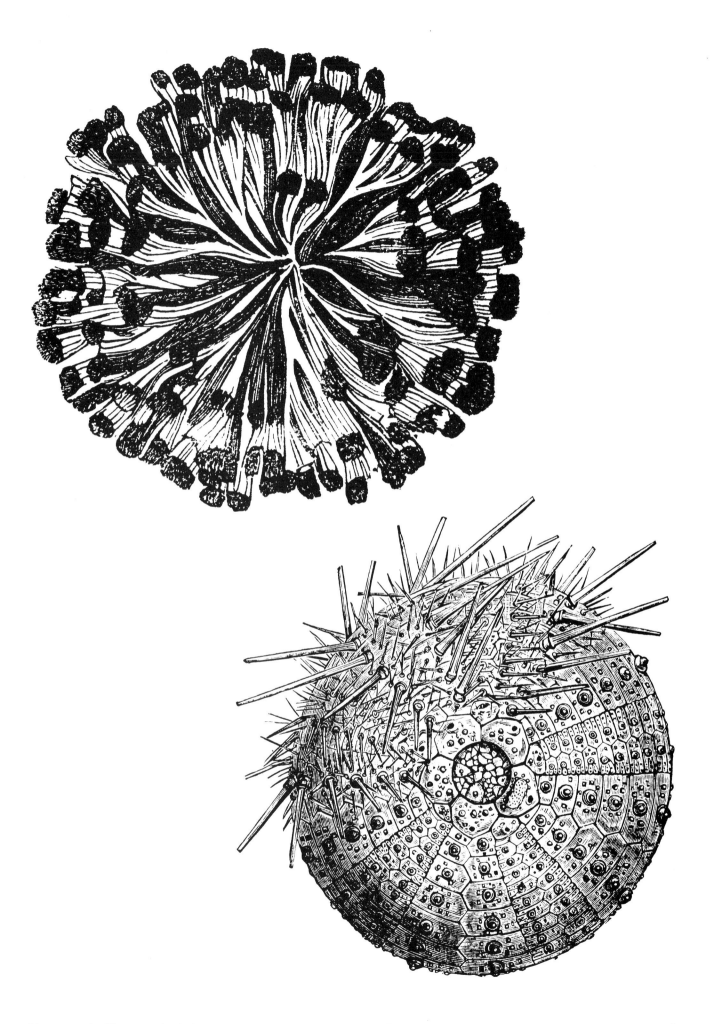

Moss coral: *Flustra avicularis*

Sea urchin, from above with most spines removed

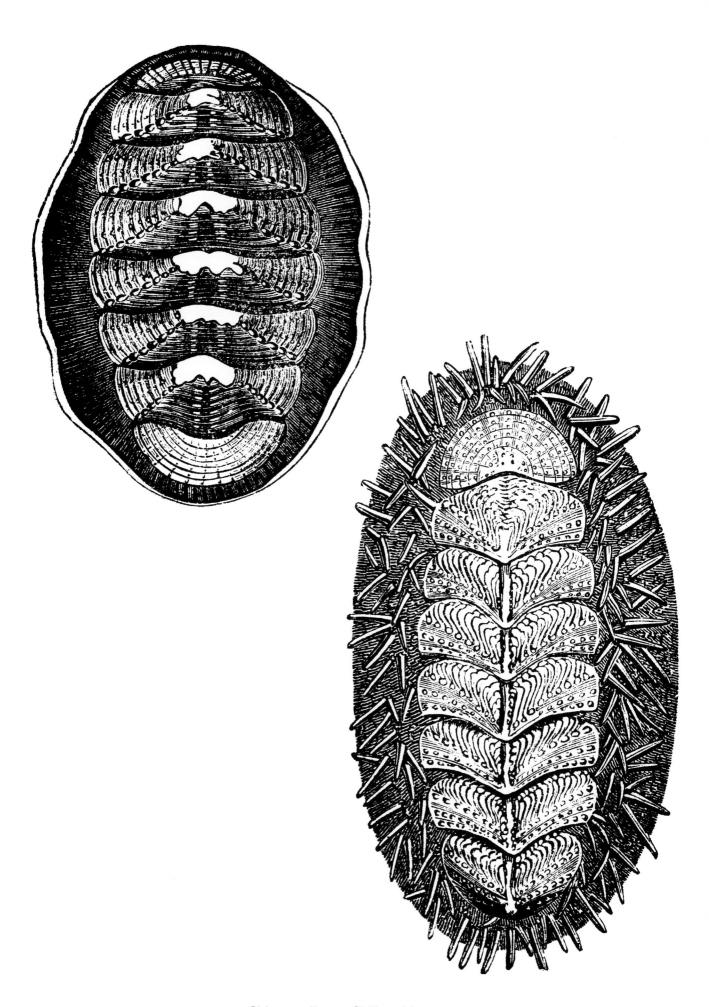

Chiton molluscs: Chilian chiton
Spiniferous chiton

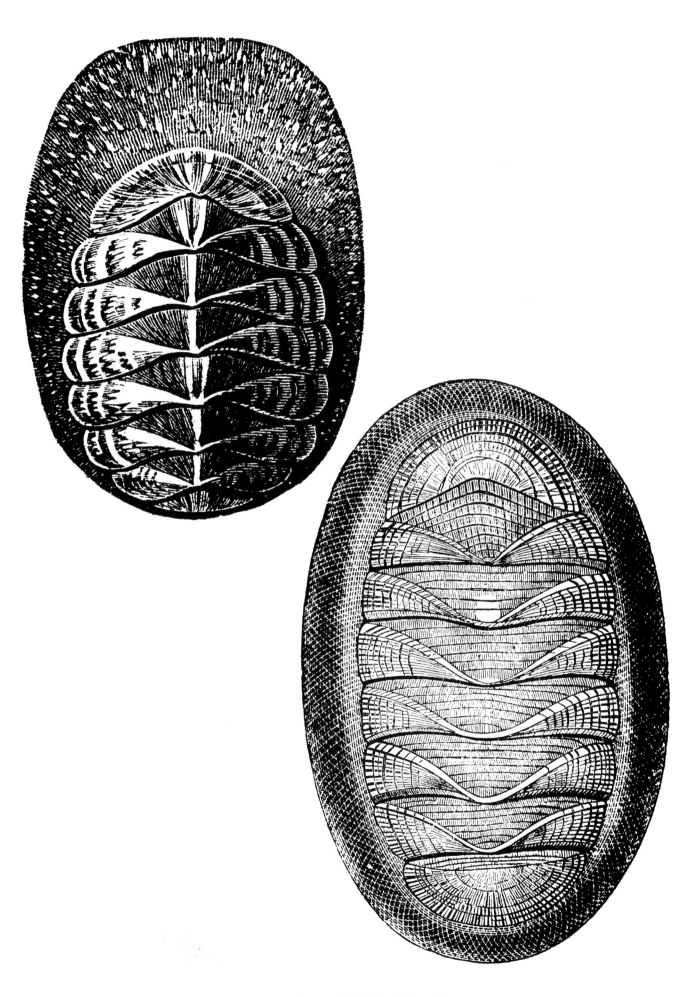

Chiton molluscs: Dr Blainville's chiton
Magnificent chiton

3

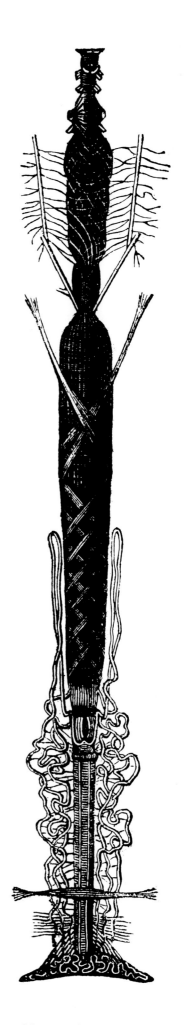

Caterpillar of tortoiseshell butterfly

Viscera of goat moth

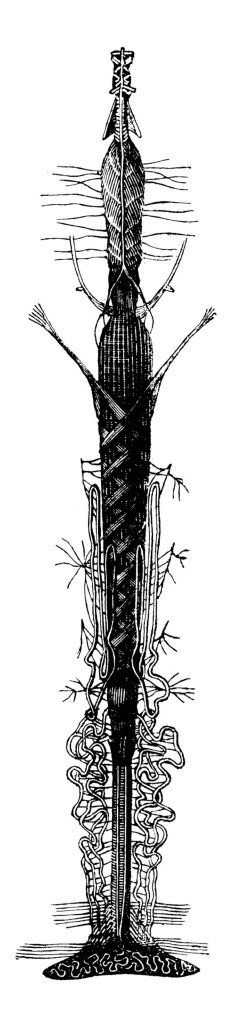

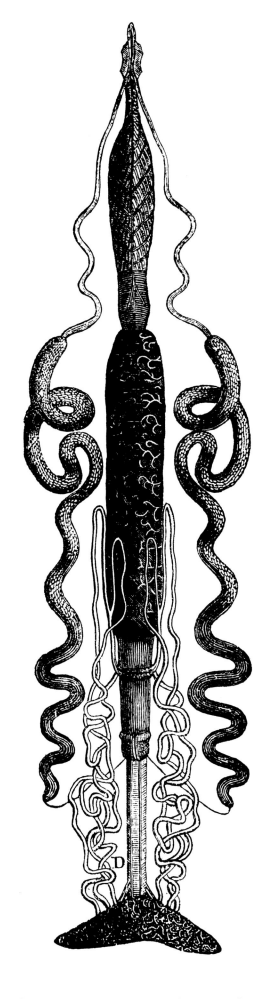

Viscera of goat moth

Organisation of caterpillar of goat moth

5

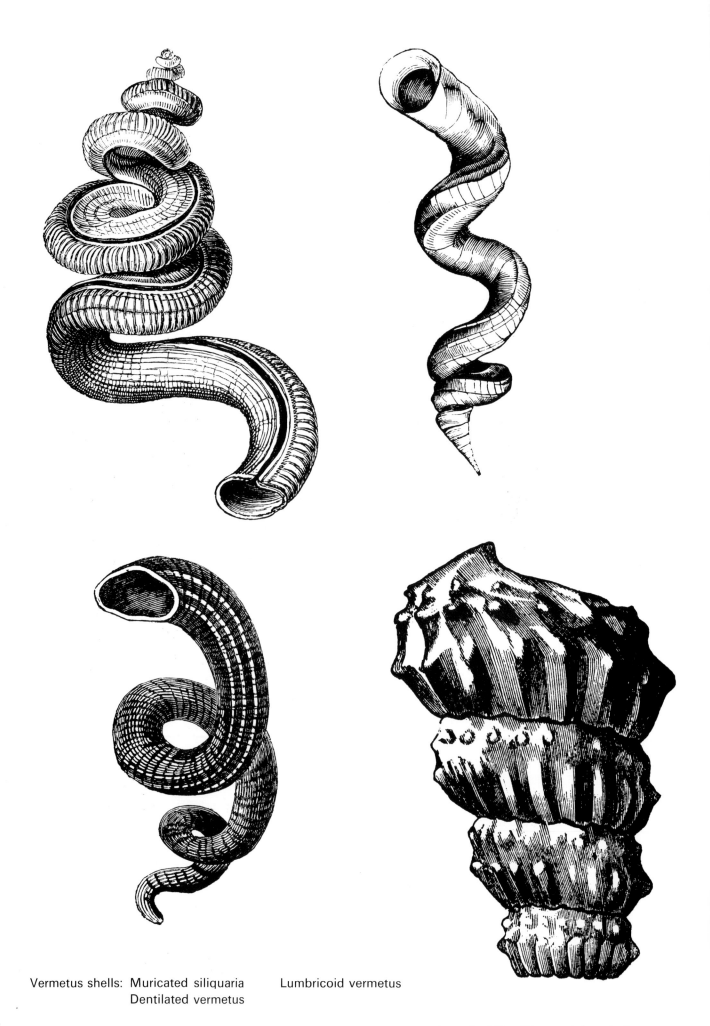

Vermetus shells: Muricated siliquaria   Lumbricoid vermetus
Dentilated vermetus

Imperfect Turrilites costatus shell

A group of vermeti

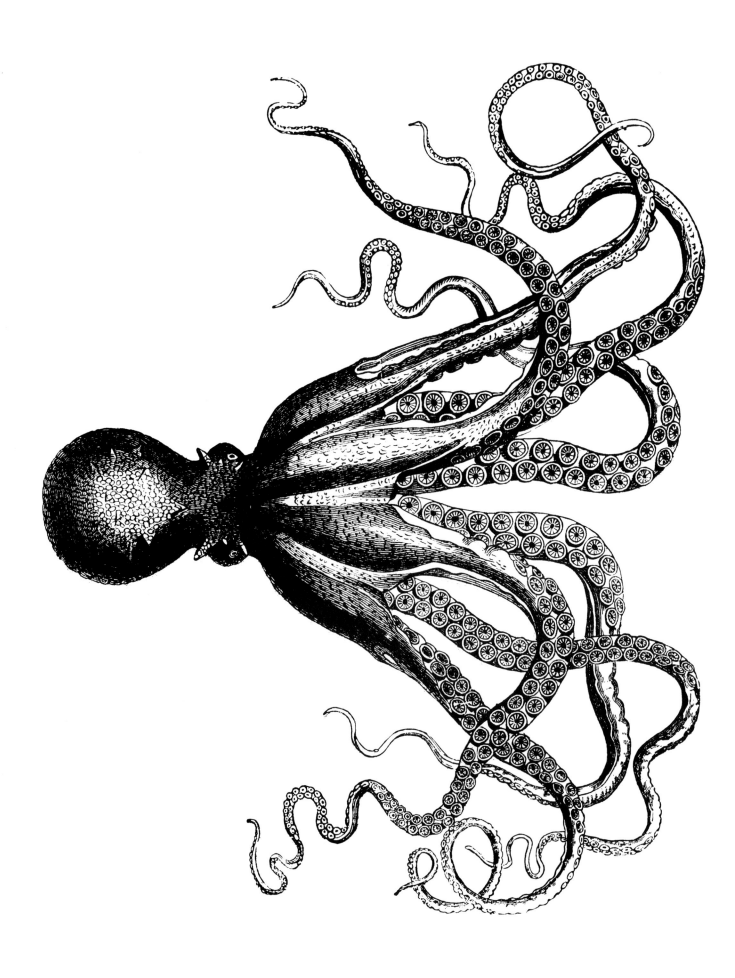

Common cuttle fish

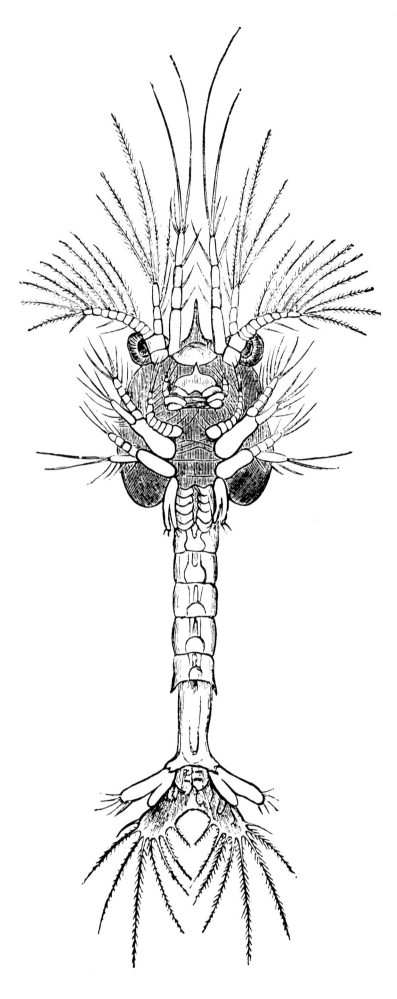

Young lobster

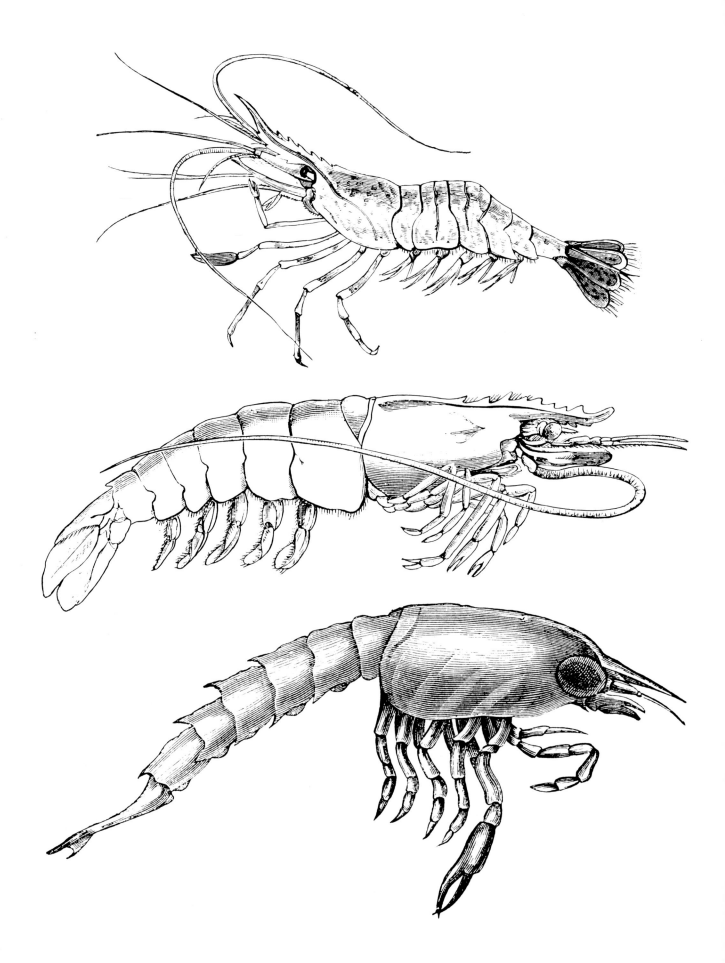

Common prawn: *Palæmon serratus*

Common shrimp

Prawn *Penœus* (mysts form)

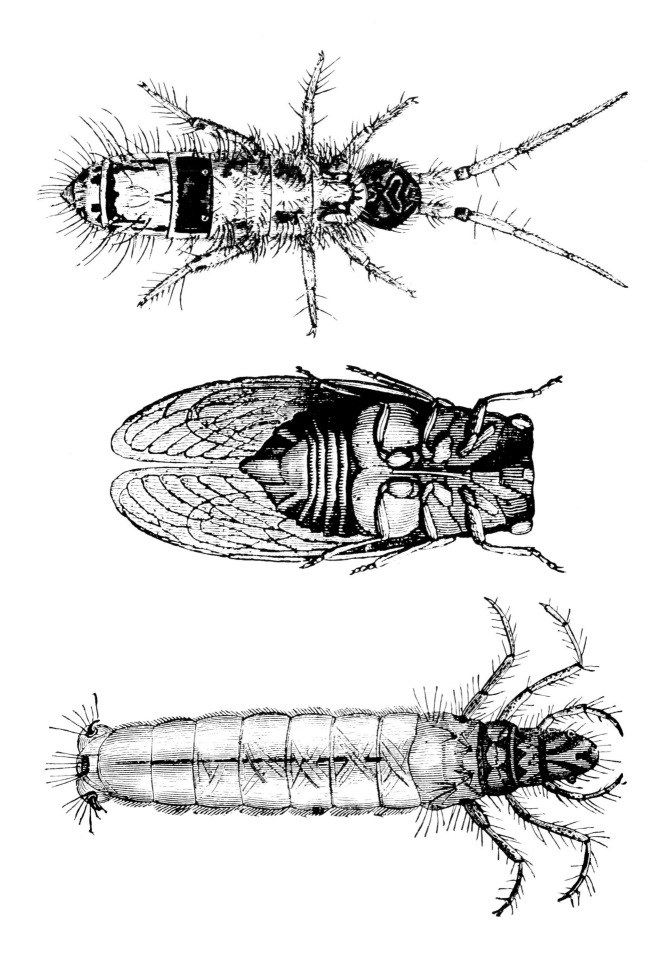

Orchesella cincta

Male cicada, underside

Lava of genus *Lymnophilus*

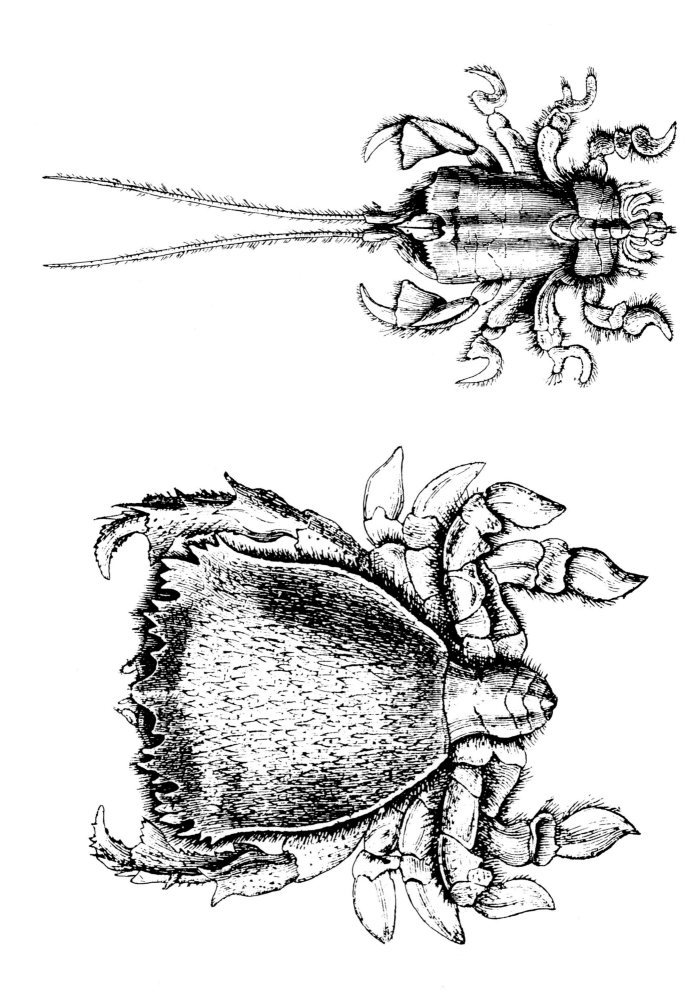

Crab: *Albunia*

Frog crab

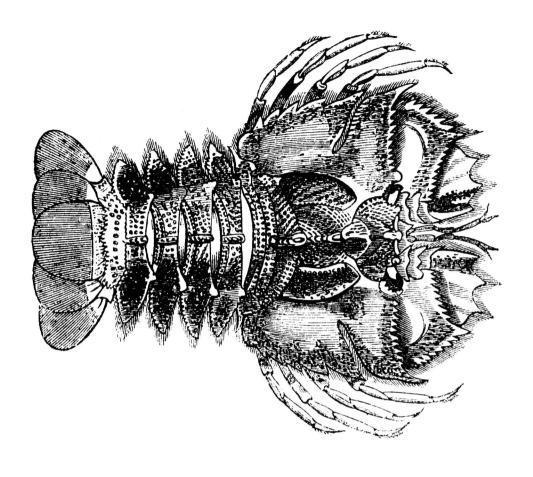

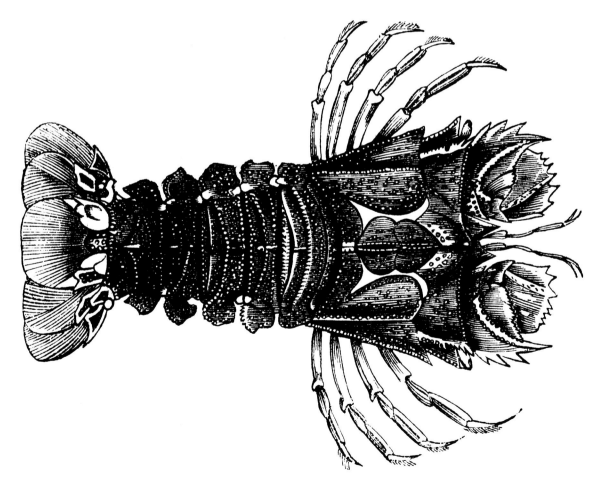

Prawns: *Ibacus peronii*
Thenus orientalis

B

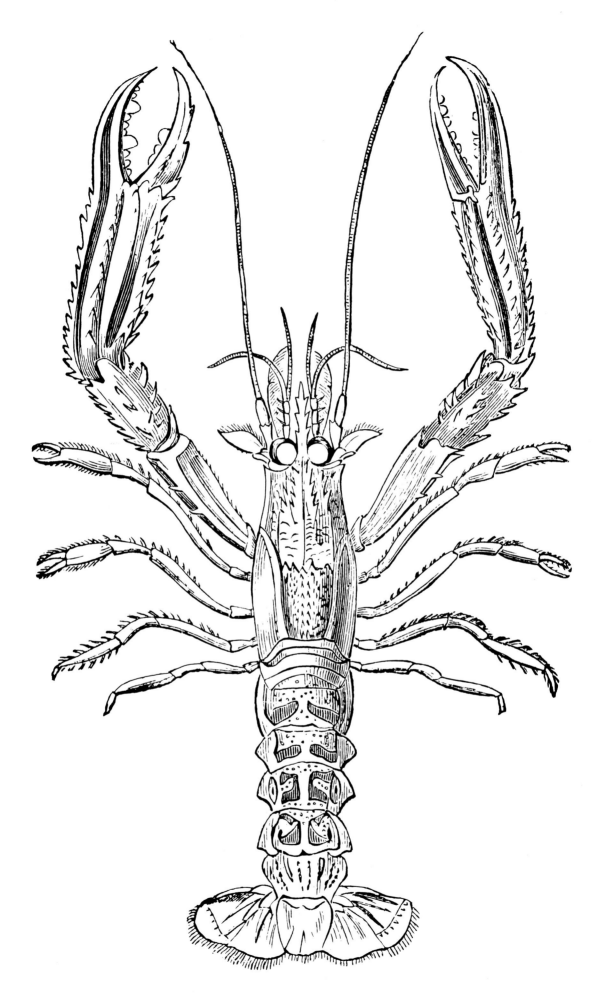

Norway lobster

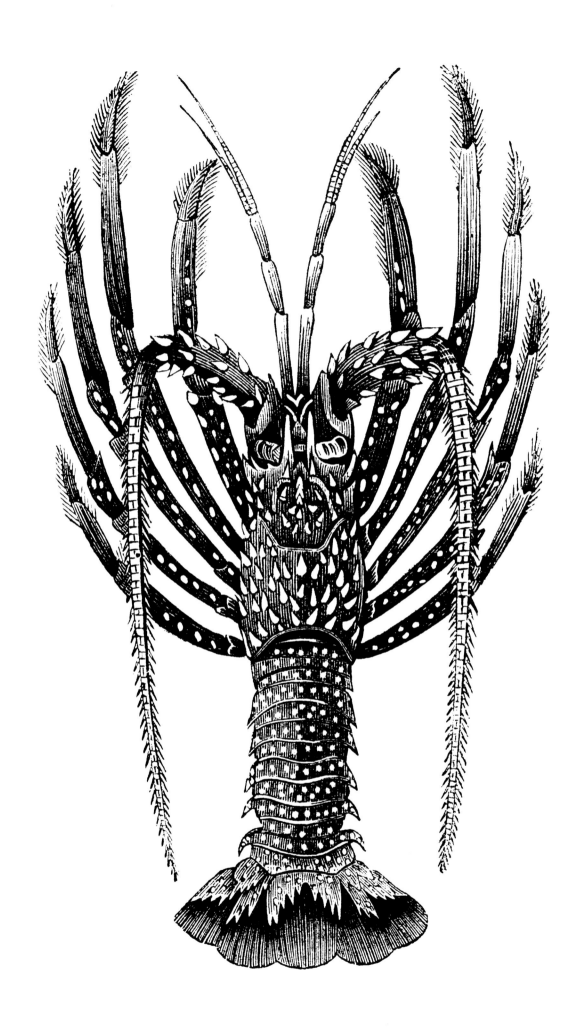

Crayfish of the Antilles

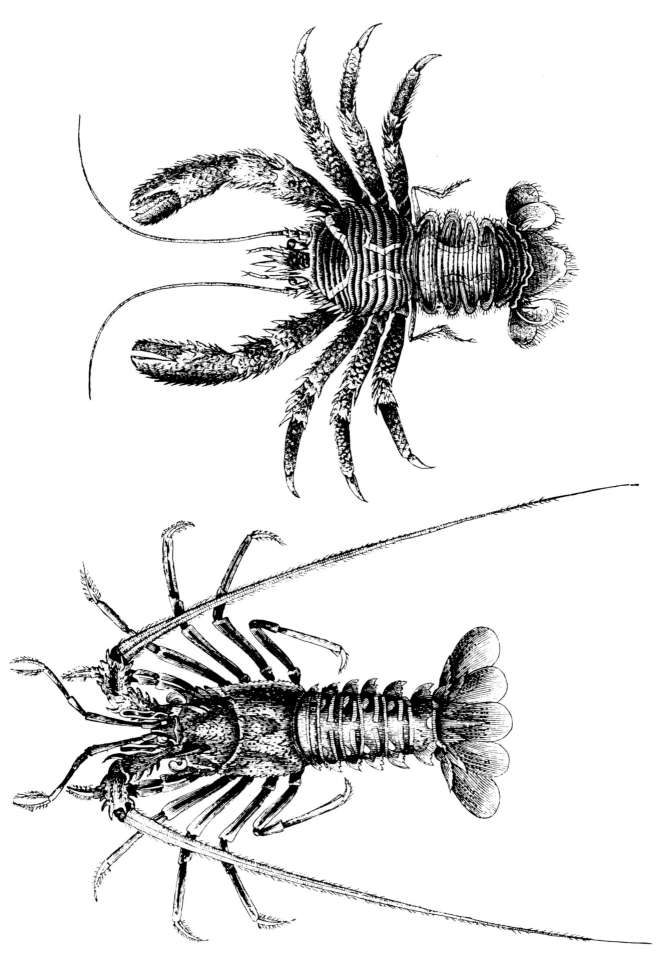

Plated lobster

Spiny lobster

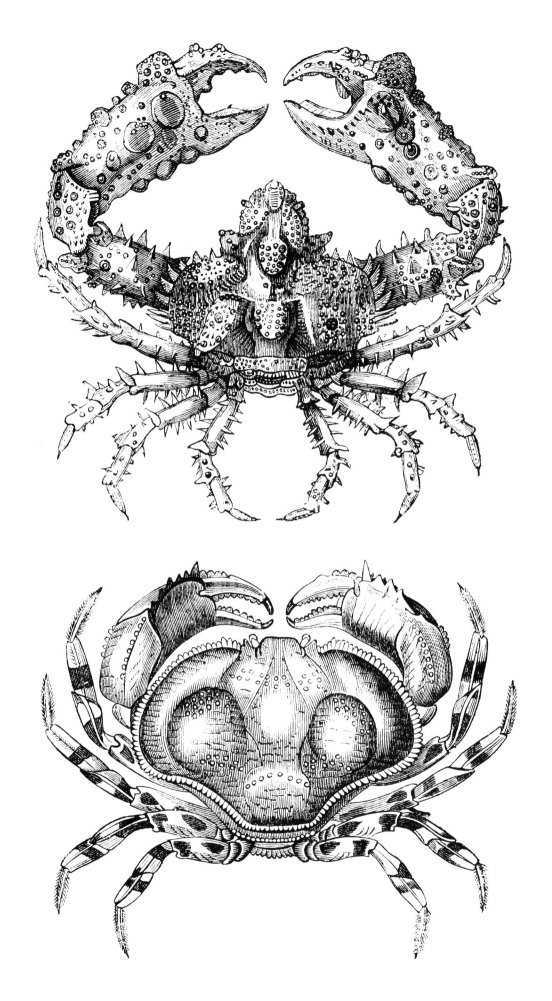

Crabs: *Parthenope horrida*
Hepatus fasciatus

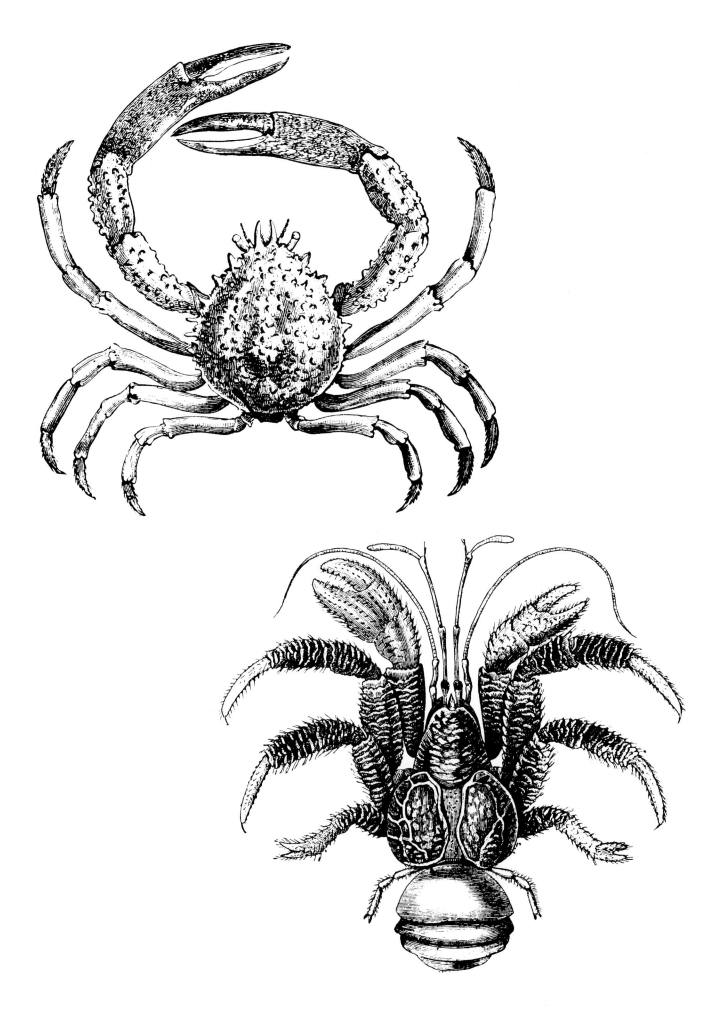

Spider crab   Purse crab

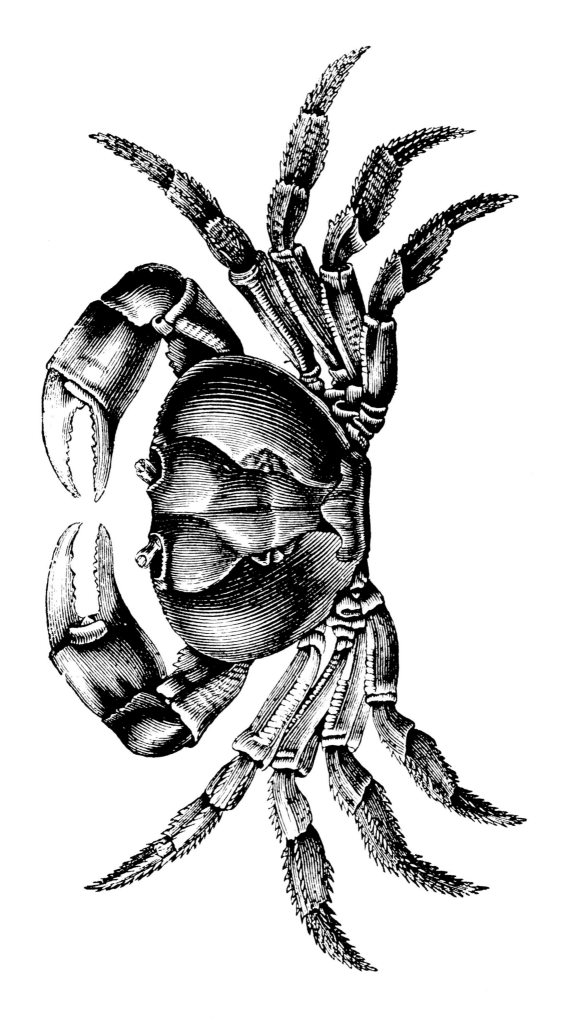

Land crab

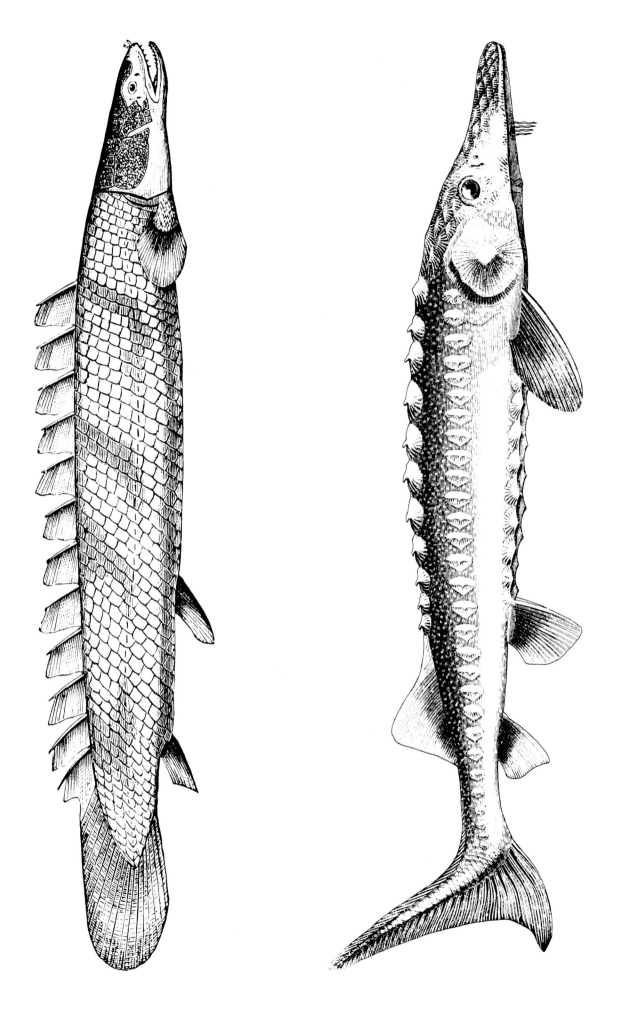

Bony pike of the Nile: *Polypterus*   Common sturgeon

Dallia pectoralis   *Cottus taeniopterus*

21

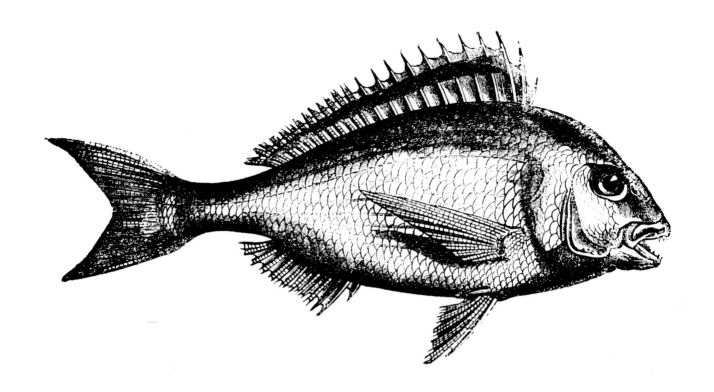

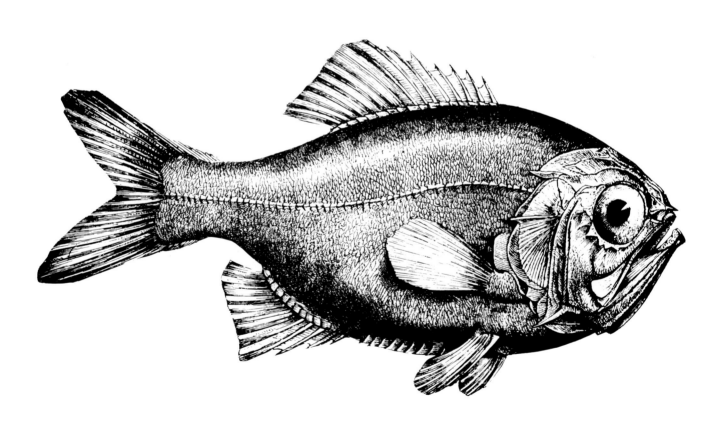

Gilt head

New Zealand trachichthis

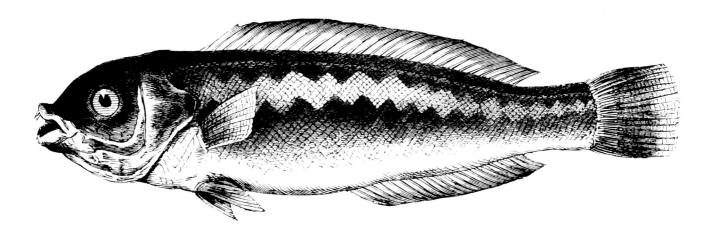

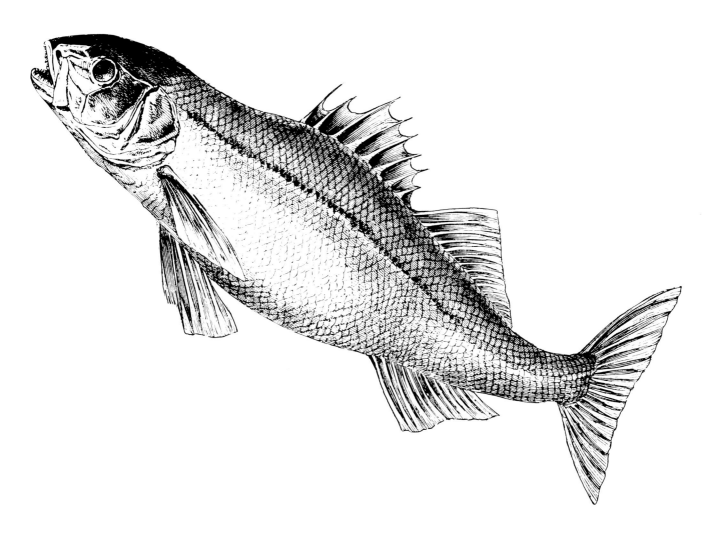

Rainbow wrasse

Bass

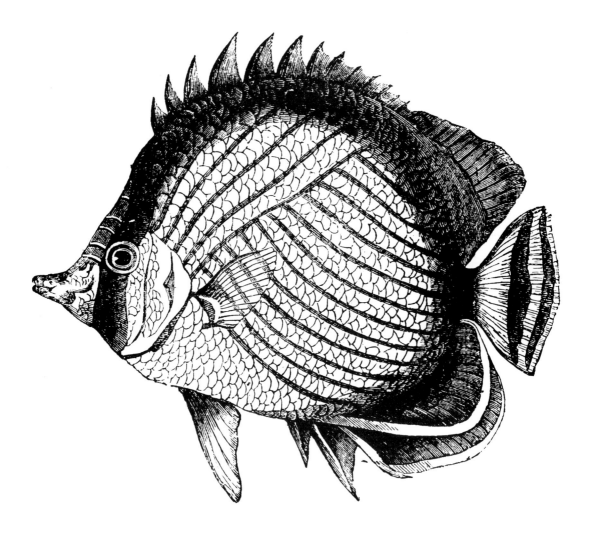

Wandering chaetodon

Pelor filamentosum

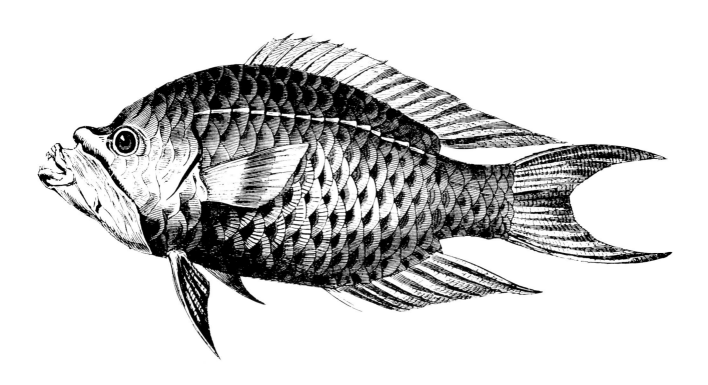

Eyed blenny

Epibulus insidiator

Ocellated *Pteraclis*   Bat chaetodon

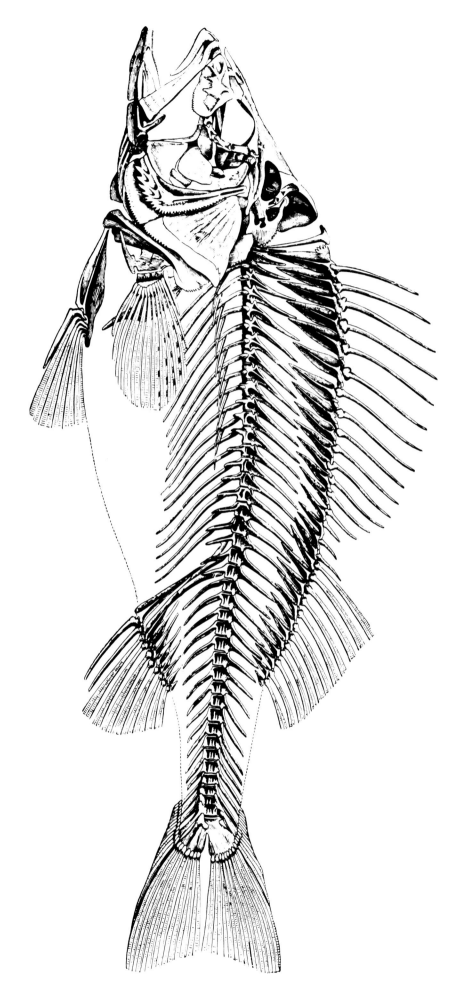

Skeleton of common perch

27

Great hornbill

The hoopoe

Pearl-spotted barbet

Chinese pheasant

Common topaz humming bird

Magpie

Californian quail

Wild turkey

32

Crested grebe

Summer or wood duck

Leptalis theonoe

Ithomia flora

Death's head hawk moth

Oleander hawk moth

Great lantern fly

35

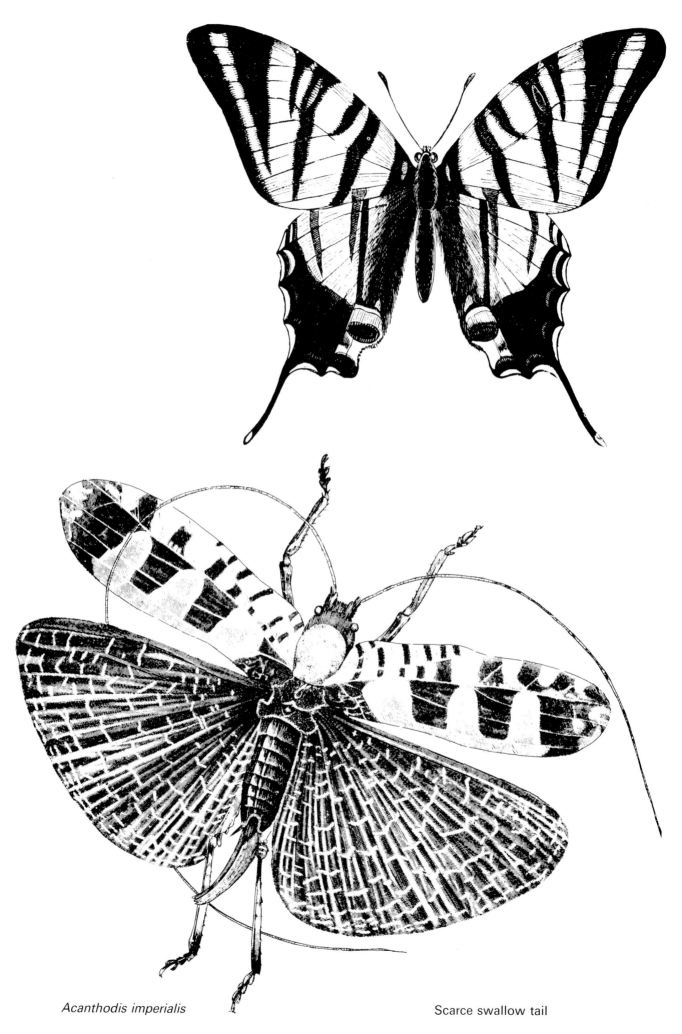

Acanthodis imperialis

Scarce swallow tail

Alucita hexadactyla

Palpares libelluloides

Papillio merope

37

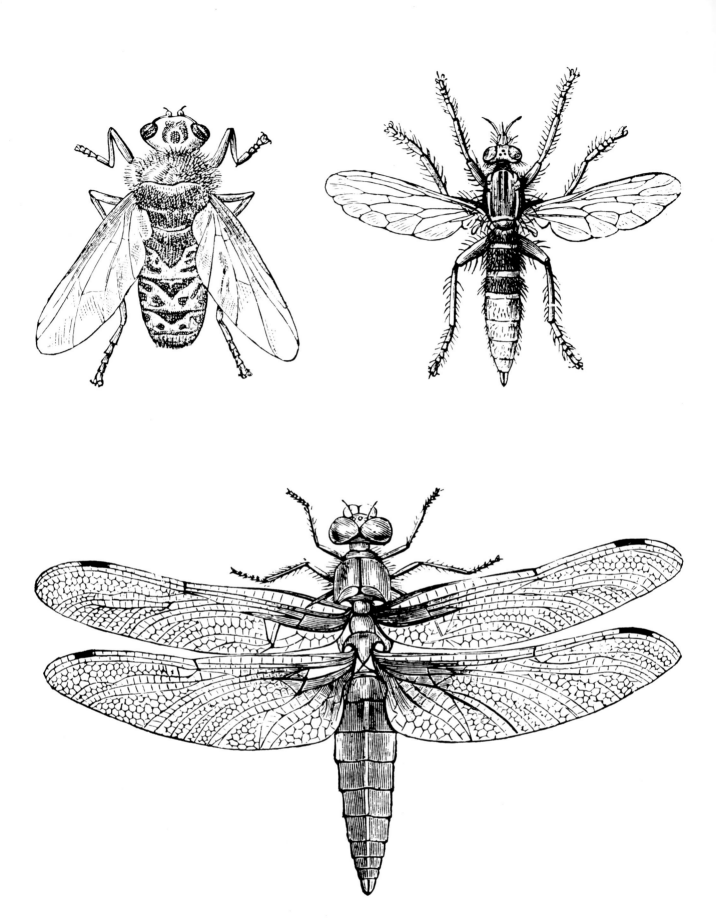

Gastrus equi

Asilus crabroniformis

Libellula depressa

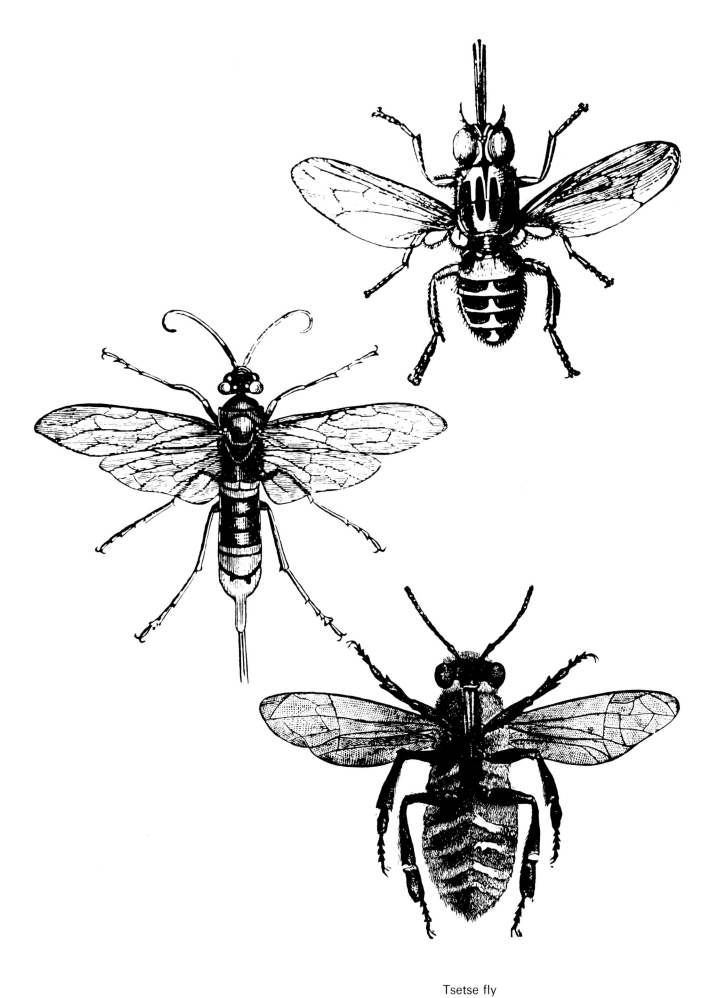

Tailed wasp: *Sirex gigas*

Tsetse fly

Bee, underside

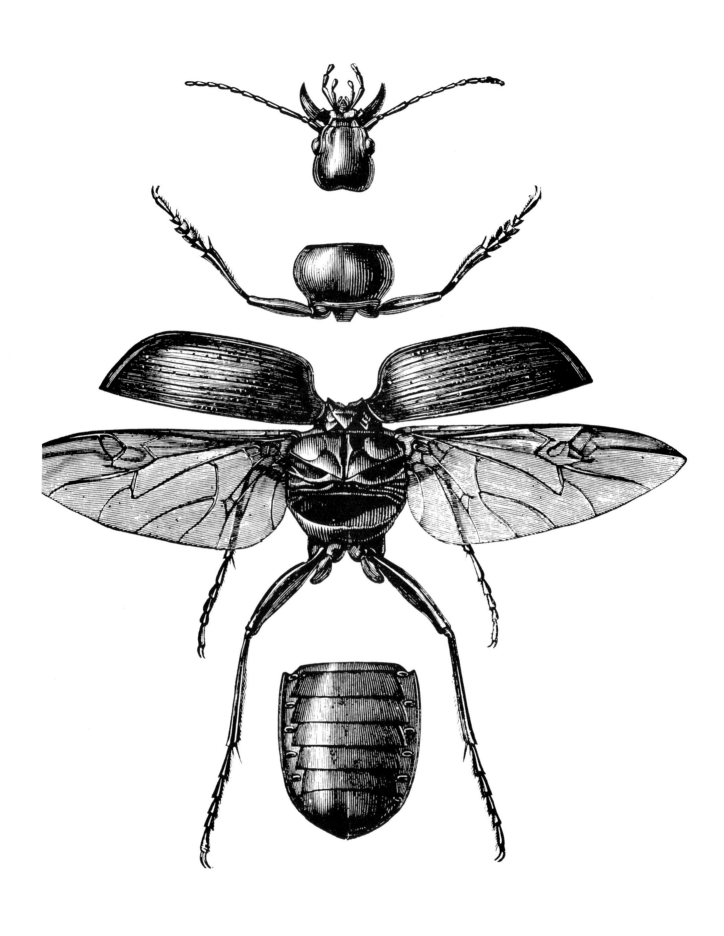

Beetle: *Calosma sycophanta* (separated)

Stag beetle

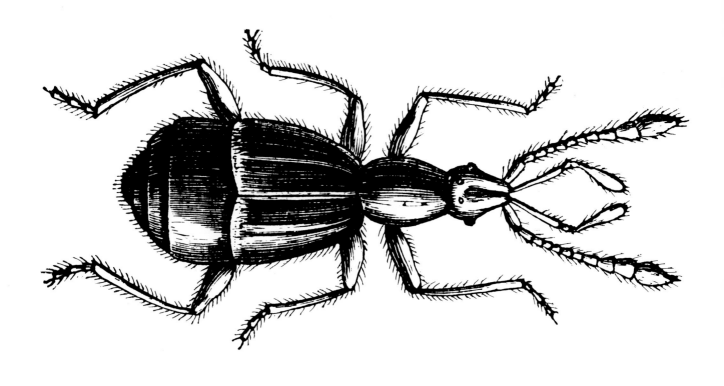

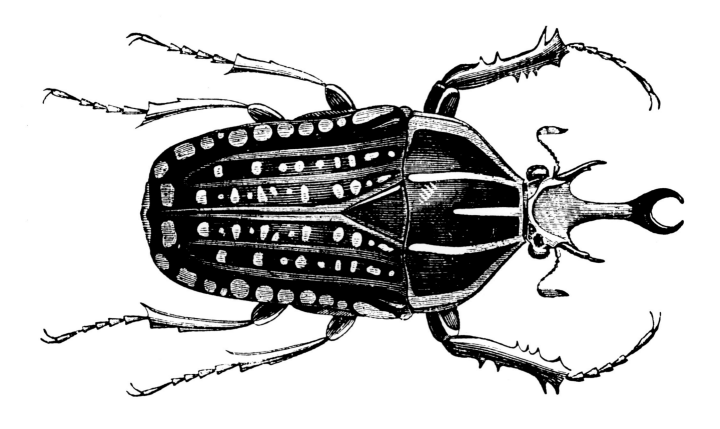

Beetles: *Pselaphus heisii*
          Ceratorhina

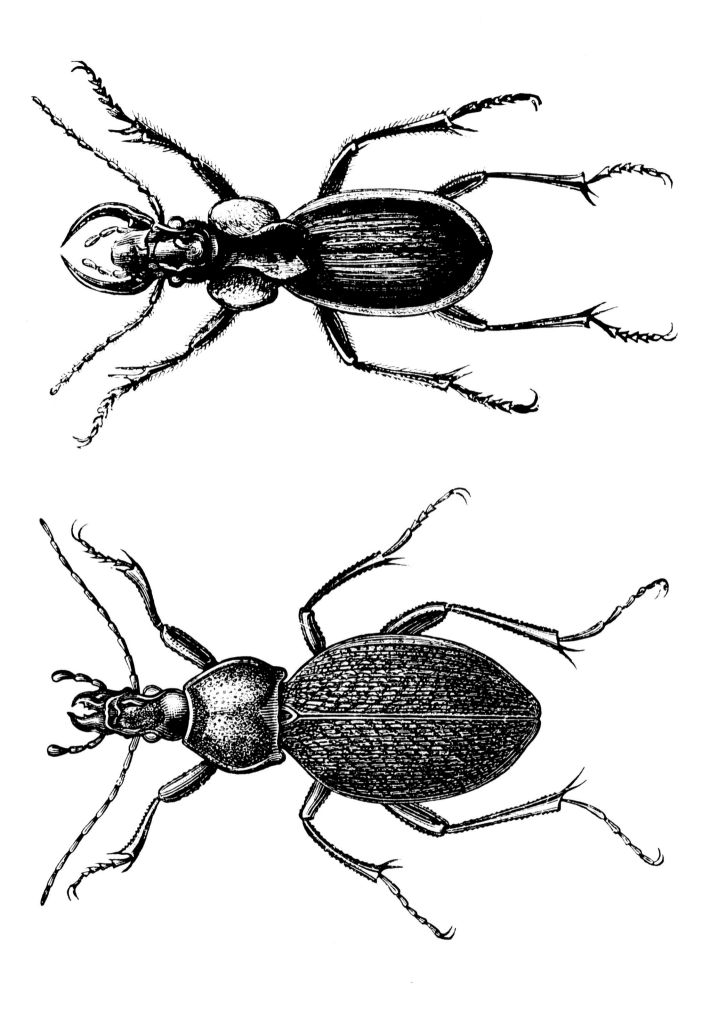

Beetles: *Procerus gigas*
Anthia thoracica

Moloch lizard

Cape girdle-tailed lizard

Rough-tailed lizard

Armed agama lizard

D

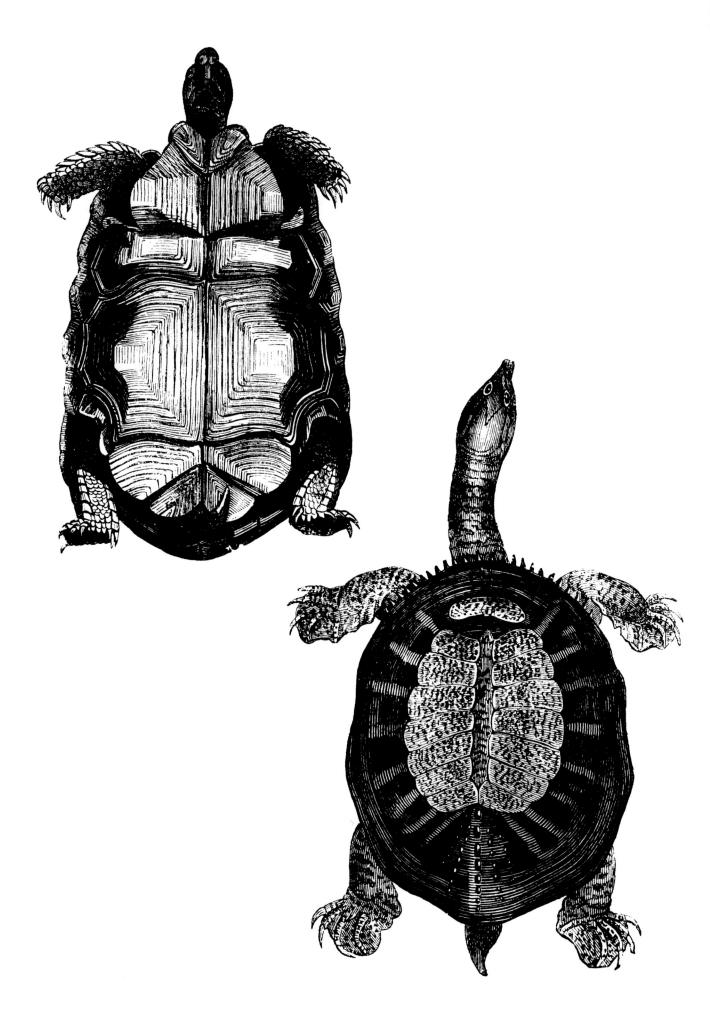

Tortoise: Arachnoid pyxis, from below

American river tortoise

Tortoises: Arachnoid pyxis, from above   New Holland chelodina

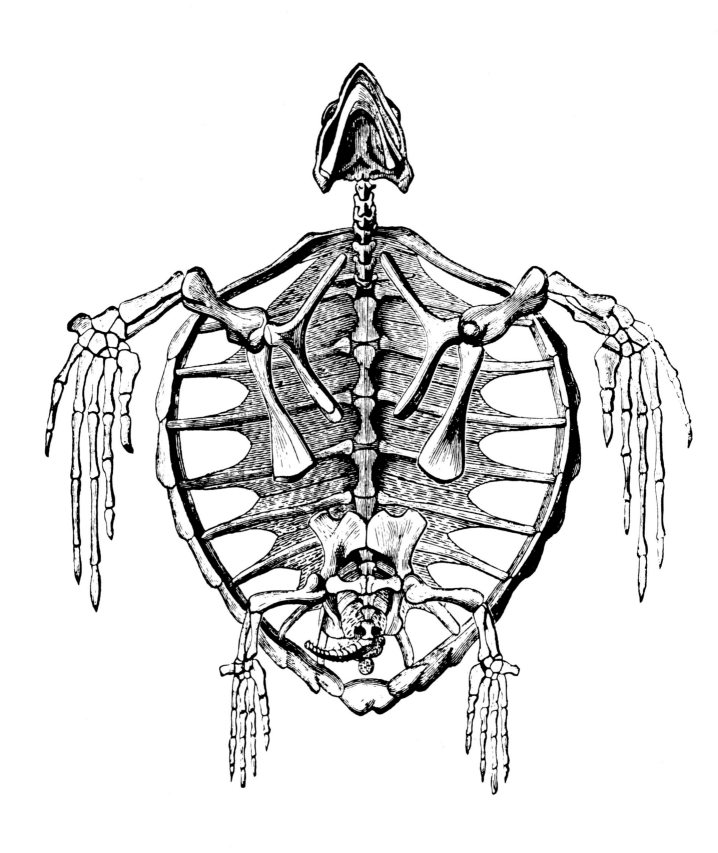

Skeleton of turtle

Spotted salamander

Common toad

Water frog

Frog: Boie's *Ceratophris*

Marbled toad

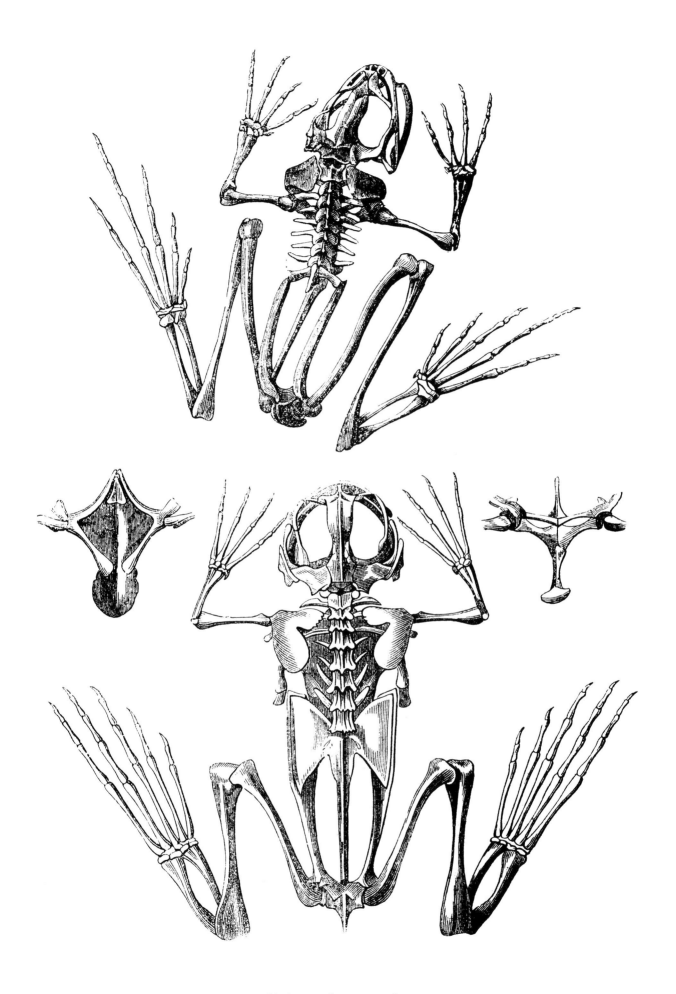

Skeleton of common frog

Skeleton of frog, Cape dactylaethra

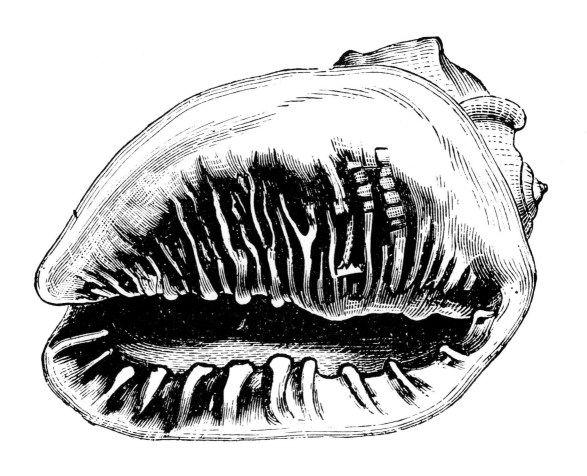

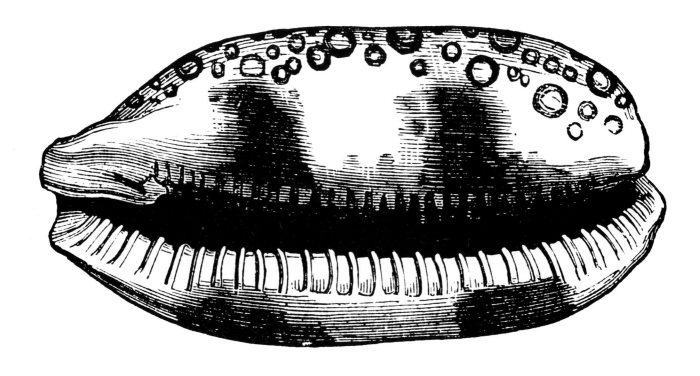

Shells: *Cassis madagascariensis*
Cowrie argus

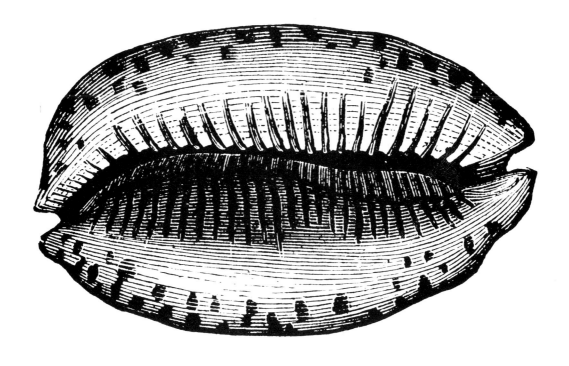

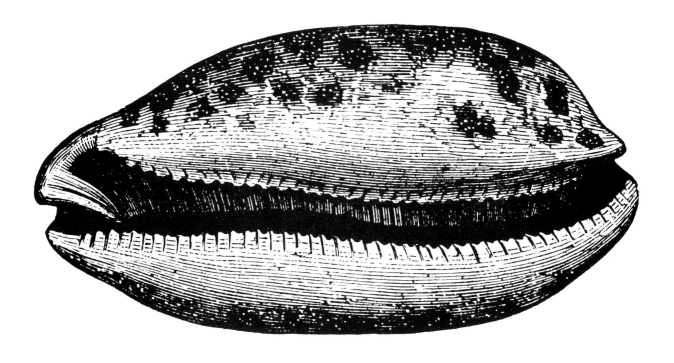

Shells: Cowrie histro
Testudinaria

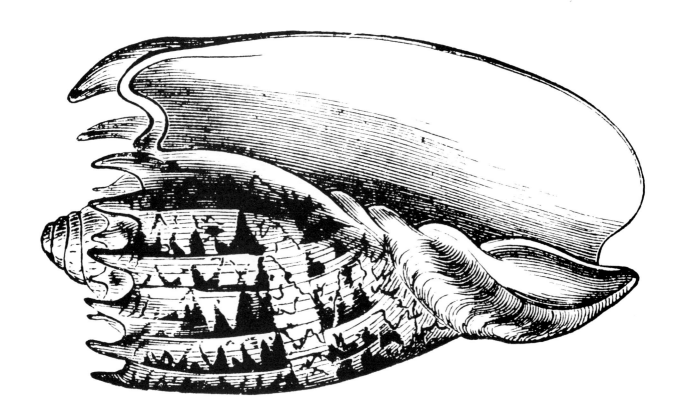

Shells: *Volute imperialis*
Harpa imperialis

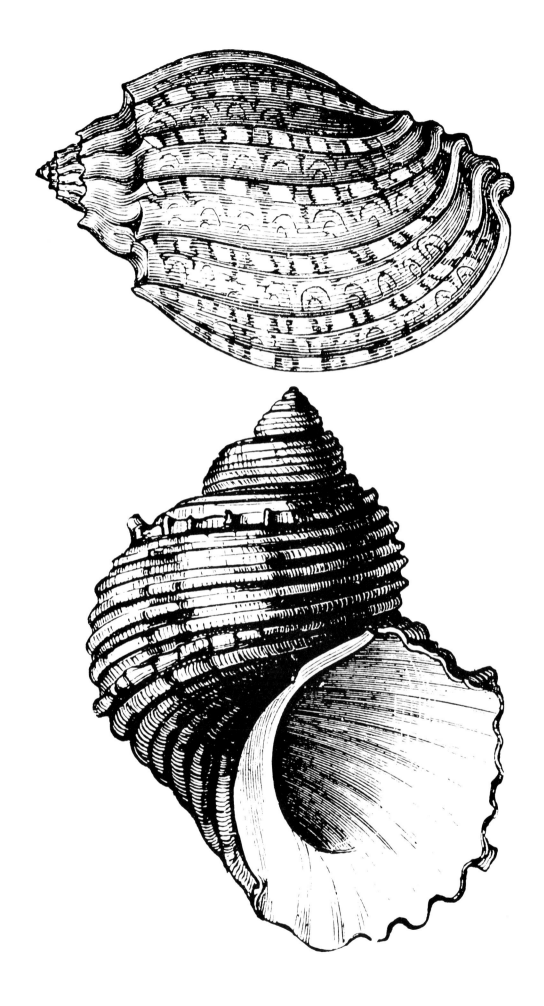

Shells: *Harpa articularis*
Turbo argyrostomus

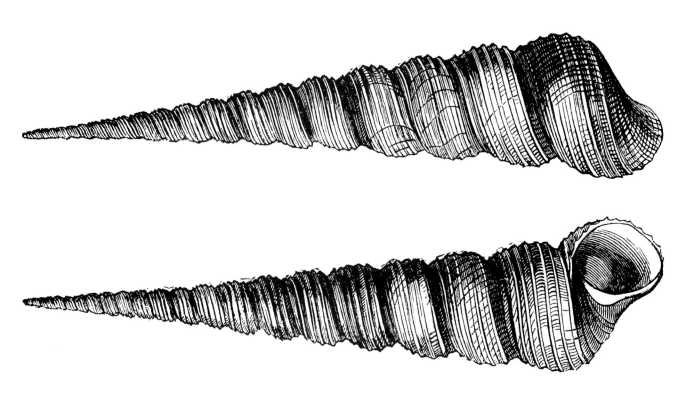

Shells: Awl-shaped *Turritella*
Marbled *Turbo*

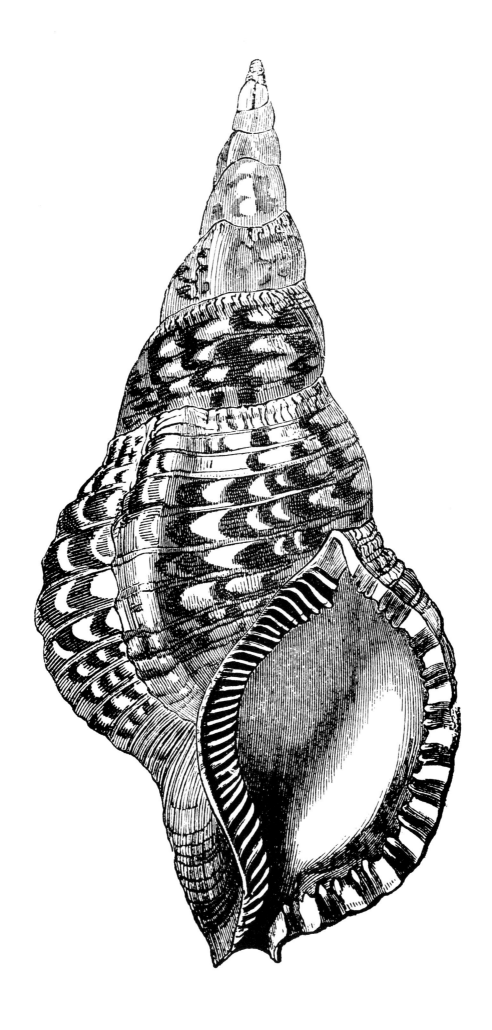

Shell: Variegated *Triton*

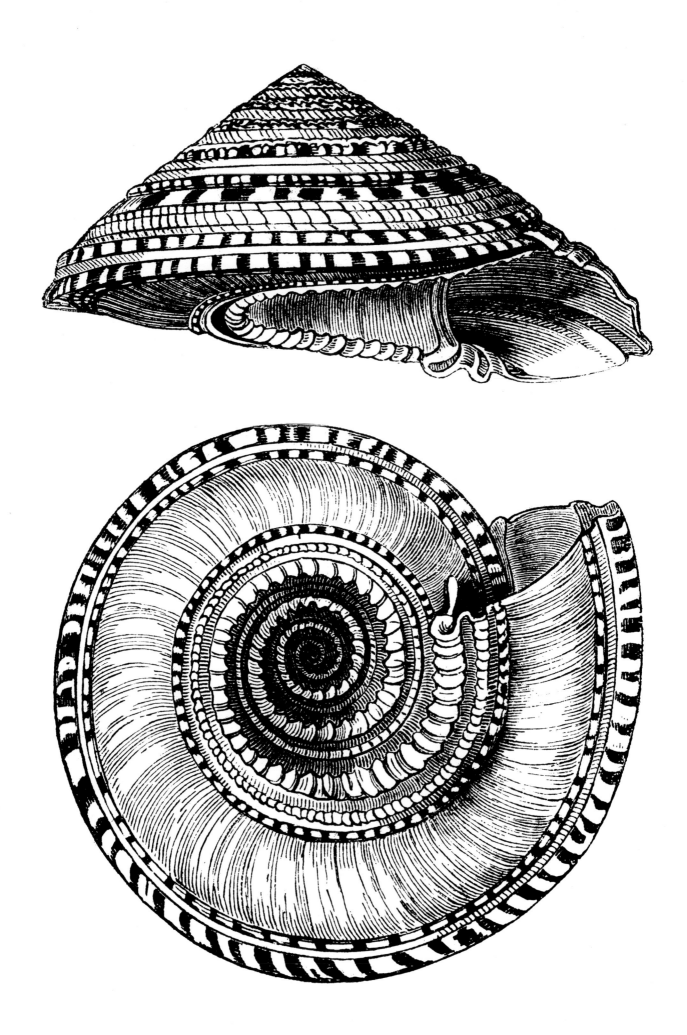

Shell: Perspective *Solarium*

Shell: Royal staircase wentletrap

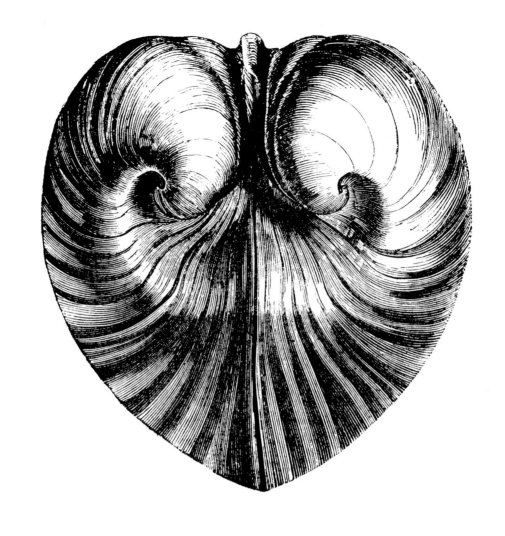

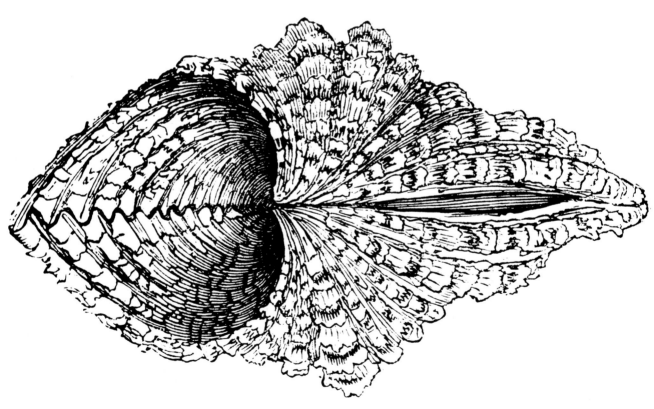

Heart *Isocardia*

Spotted *Tridacna*